Emotional Intelligence

-

Be Mindful

LEWIS ALERSON
Copyright © 2017 Lewis Alerson

All rights reserved.

EMOTIONAL INTELLIGENCE

© Copyright 2017 by Lewis Alerson - All rights reserved.

This document is geared towards providing exact and reliable information in regard to the topic and issue covered. The publication is sold on the idea that the publisher is not required to render accounting, officially permitted, or otherwise, qualified services. If advice is necessary, legal or professional, a practised individual in the profession should be ordered.

- From a Declaration of Principles which was accepted and approved equally by a Committee of the American Bar Association and a Committee of Publishers and Associations.

In no way is it legal to reproduce, duplicate, or transmit any part of this document by either electronic means or in printed format. Recording of this publication is strictly prohibited, and any storage of this document is not allowed unless with written permission from the publisher. All rights reserved.

The information provided herein is stated to be truthful and consistent, in that any liability, in terms of inattention or otherwise, by any usage or abuse of any policies, processes, or directions contained within is the solitary and utter responsibility of the recipient reader. Under no circumstances will any legal responsibility or blame be held against the publisher for any reparation, damages, or monetary loss due to the information herein, either directly or indirectly.

Respective authors own all copyrights not held by the publisher.

The information herein is offered for informational purposes solely and is universal as so. The presentation of the information is without a contract or any type of guarantee assurance.

The trademarks that are used are without any consent, and the publication of the trademark is without permission or backing by the trademark owner. All trademarks and brands within this book are for clarifying purposes only and are the owned by the owners themselves, not affiliated with this document.

CONTENTS

	Introduction	Pg 4
1	Basics of Emotional Intelligence	Pg 5
2	Understanding Your Emotions	Pg 10
3	Manage Your Life with Emotional Intelligence	Pg 16
4	Understanding Emotions in Others	Pg 21
5	Changing Emotions in Others	Pg 25
	Conclusion	Pg 28

INTRODUCTION

Firstly, congratulations on getting your copy of Emotional Intelligence: Be Mindful. I would like to show my appreciation by offering you 3 free copies of my other self-help books.

Simply visit www.rebrand.ly/3books

Grab them today before it's potentially gone tomorrow. I hope you enjoy it and are able to benefit from it. Now let's get back to the topic of Emotional Intelligence.

The following chapters will discuss some of the many ways mastering our emotional intelligence can improve our lives. The course of our personal history heavily relies on what happens to us, but more importantly, how we react to it. When bad things happen, we can choose to wallow in it or dust ourselves off and start again, and mastering our emotions is key to doing the latter.

You will discover how important it is to understand where your emotions stem from to make an important positive change in your life. Understanding your frustrations, fears, and happiness can guide us to making decisions for the rest of our lives.

There are plenty of books on this subject on the market, thanks again for choosing this one! Every effort was made to ensure it is full of as much useful information as possible. I hope you enjoy it!

1 | BASICS OF EMOTIONAL INTELLIGENCE

Emotional intelligence is the ability to understand your emotions and have the functional capacity to control your feelings and change the way you react to any given set of emotions. Someone who is highly intelligent emotionally is generally even-keeled and does not fall victim to extreme emotional outbursts. This person is likely highly successful socially and professionally.

Studies show that higher levels of emotional intelligence correspond to more outstanding personal relationships and social interactions. As we know, these skills are the building blocks of everything else in life, including marriage, friendships, work relationships and overall success. Interestingly, some research finds that people with higher levels of emotional intelligence are more successful than people with a high IQ, but low emotional intelligence scores. This is likely because they are book smart but unable to effectively manage relationships well enough to put that information into practice. This is equivalent to knowing everything about your line of work, but nobody can stand you because you are abrasive and bad at communicating. Nothing can actually be done unless you have the connections to make it happen.

Everyone is born with an inherent need to connect with others. For some, this comes very easily, and they are in good connection with their feelings and empathise with others. For many more people, this is a learned skill, something that requires conscious effort to build over time.

Studies also show that emotional education in the form of classes and a conscious effort to recognise and understand feelings will raise a low emotional intelligence score. Emotional intelligence comes with a great deal of time and practice. It is something that needs to be nurtured constantly, always learning more about yourself and growing your emotions. While it may be difficult to find a self-help class set up in your area, you can certainly work on enhancing your emotional intelligence on your own, knowing that there is such a thing.

Emotional intelligence is measured in some ways, but the most common method is with a Multifactorial Emotional Intelligence Scale (MEIS) test. In the past, tests like this that have measured reactions and emotional response given questions about themselves have been used to help diagnose mental disorders, depression, and anxiety, among other things. These written tests help a person focus in on and reflect on their own emotional health using guided questioning about all aspects of emotional intelligence. These are the ability to recognise emotions, to control emotions, to recognise emotion in others and to respond appropriately.

Most questions are not questions at all, but a statement and the person must answer with on a 'true,' 'sometimes true,' 'not true' scale. For example, the statement, "I find myself worrying about everything, big problems and small," may be answered by agreeing or not agreeing about this specific personality trait.

As these questions are answered based on each person's personality, there are no right and wrong answers. Instead, the answers can only be grouped to show common traits and problems. There is no one perfect, desirable personality, and every person has strengths and weaknesses. Perhaps one person is very sociable, with many friends, but is incapable of getting in touch with their emotions. This may lead them to be a people-pleaser, considering the needs and emotions of others ahead of their own.

On the contrary, a person considered antisocial and has only a few friends may be really good at understanding their own needs, but not of others. They prefer to be alone, as this is an emotionally stable place, but do not lack the empathy to connect well with others. Both people have their strengths and flaws.

What any type of emotional intelligence testing can do is pinpoint some areas that may need attention. For example, the person who has a hard time connecting with others may need to learn and develop new social skills to enhance their social life.

Unfortunately, the results of some of this testing may seem like common sense. If you have ever done any amount of self-reflection, this test will probably not be able to tell you something you did not already know. Most likely, you have noticed areas of your life that need attention because they have given you problems. Therefore, it is not necessary to get any testing done to grow your emotional intelligence. More on how to recognise these things in the following chapter.

Learning to work with your emotions can have a huge impact on your life. From the standpoint of overall happiness, being in touch with your emotions can help you make decisions that point you in the right direction, instead of always circling back toward habits that only bring you sadness or anger.

For example, your current thought process could be focused on monetary gain. For most people, having enough money is an issue, and for all, it is something that certainly cannot be ignored. Financial security makes everyone feel more safe and happy, regardless of the fact that money itself cannot make us happy. However, chasing money instead of doing things that make you happy will ultimately lead to negative emotions.

In search of wealth, you may take jobs you do not like and schmooze with people you are uncomfortable with just to make a buck. Your decisions are driven solely by the bottom line, not on your emotional well-being. Instead, choosing a career path or job based on your overall happiness is a much better idea. Instead of circling the unhappy drain, you can lift yourself up and above your negative emotions and find out what truly makes you happy. When you choose to do a job that excites you and makes you feel accomplished, you will shine, and the money will follow.

Getting out of bad habits with familiar people is another area that lots of people need to work on. Most people can say that they have been in at least one bad relationship. This may have been with a friend, romantic partner or family member. Sticking with a relationship to simply keep up the status is faulty. Ignoring signs of manipulation, jealousy or greed for the sake of having someone in your life will lead to nothing but negative emotions in the future. When it comes to family it is important to not let go of that relationship, as it is possible to maintain your distance and not let go of the relationship. Setting boundaries will likely be difficult, but do your best to maintain civility.

Getting in touch with your inner self and determining what it is you need emotionally will save you much time in the future. There are billions of people on this planet, and there is a good chance that you will just not get along with all of them. Sticking to someone who makes you feel worthless, jealous or sad is just not worth the time. Take the time to understand what it is that you need out of a relationship. On the flip side, knowing that you may not be what another person is looking for can help you let go of a negative relationship.

If you know that both of you would be better off without each other, don't be afraid to end a relationship. Being emotionally intelligent enough to understand this takes a serious amount of growth, and will still likely hurt to admit, but doing so can open doors to possibilities you did not even know existed.

Understanding yourself is one thing, but interpreting the emotions of another person can be even more difficult. It takes a great deal of time and energy to understand the emotions and needs of another person fully, but if you can begin to master these techniques, you will be unstoppable both in your personal and professional life.

Knowing people is really the cornerstone of any managerial position. It requires the ability to know what the company needs, and what your employees need. On any given day, each member of your team could be happy, upset or simply content with the way you operate things. Granted, you cannot make everybody happy, but if you can interpret the reactions your employees have to your decisions, it can help guide you going forward. For example, say you ask your team to stay late to help finish up a project for a very important client. This can go one of two ways: One, they will willingly agree, understanding how important the project is. Two, they begrudgingly stay, but voice concerns of needing to pick up their kids and how tired they feel.

While it is necessary to make executive decisions that may not always be popular, your next move can be based on the emotional feedback provided by the team. For example, if the team was gung-ho about staying, it shows that they are committed to you, that they are content with going the extra mile. It implies that you, as manager, are doing your job properly. While it may be a good idea to give some additional warning next time, running things this way will likely continue to work.

On the other hand, if your employees begrudgingly stayed, you can determine the next course of action based on their emotional response. They may not have said anything at all, but their body language says they do not think you appreciate their time or commitments outside of work. Ignoring this for the greater good of the company will have your employees hating you and your productivity slowing to a crawl. If you truly feel empathy for these people, offering an incentive, or simply asking if and when it would be appropriate to work late would go a long way to show that you are in touch with their needs.

It really is amazing how beneficial it can be to tap into your own emotional needs and understand the feelings of others. This can help you across all aspects of your life to make changes for the good. The following chapters will each be dedicated to a pillar of emotional intelligence, delving deeper into the science behind each, and giving specific examples of how to get in better touch with emotions and act upon them in appropriate ways. Your mind can be in control of your emotions if you teach it to be.

2 | UNDERSTANDING YOUR EMOTIONS

If the title of this chapter evokes images of crying over your breakfast cereal about every little insignificant episode of your life, don't worry. Getting in touch with your emotions does not mean that you need to be outwardly emotional. This is good news, as many people are withdrawn about showing emotion, and the idea of sharing their feelings with others and wearing them on their sleeves is far from appetising.

You are at the centre of your emotions, and it is important to explore them within yourself to understand them fully. Of course, getting an alternative perspective from a third party like a therapist or trusted friend can help you sort out the root causes of your emotions, but you know yourself better than anyone. You will likely be more comfortable exploring your emotions internally first.

So, where do we start? How can you suddenly just be in touch with your thoughts, feelings, and emotions? Simply, you cannot. This is a process that takes a bit of practice to master. More likely than not, your emotional life has been put on the back burner, cast aside for more important things like making money, living a socially acceptable life, and the like. Your emotions have probably not been front and centre since you learned as a child to squash those emotions and just do what you are told.

It is not that you do not have emotions, just that you have been trained to ignore them for the sake of fitting in and obeying your elders. That, right there, was your first hour of therapy. Understanding this fact can help us uncover our old emotions, which have certainly not gone away.

There are many exercises we can try to become more at one with our emotional selves. The ideal exercise will vary by person but could include meditation, exercise, talk therapy, or even just sit quietly. No matter what you call it, investing in quiet time to simply reflect on your current and past emotions is crucial. Let's say that meditation is your first attempt at emotional awareness. Simply sit quietly and comfortably in a dimly lit room to get started. There should be no distractions, so that you may just concentrate on the task at hand.

This task may feel completely foreign to you, as you normally rush through life, getting things done, avoiding how you are feeling. Just sit back, focus on your breath for a few moments, then ask yourself how you are feeling. Avoid answering your own questions with the typical, "I feel fine," "I'm okay" pleasantries you would use on the street. Give a reason you feel fine, or why you are having a bad day. Elaborate, explore the feelings.

For example, your answer may be that you are feeling overwhelmed. It is completely normal to feel this way, and the worst thing to do right now is to push that feeling away. Just sit with it for a few minutes. Allow the stress to shine through, Feel it all over your body. Feelings are natural, not to be squashed entirely. You must feel them begin to understand why it is you feel them in the first place.

Logically, you would next respond with why you feel this way, even giving a list of reasons. While this particular part of the exercise may make you feel even more overwhelmed, taking the next step is crucial to alleviating it. The next step is to rationalise your feelings of anxiety logically. I bet you cannot.

Most stresses and anxieties in life are unwarranted. We worry about small things that have no real consequence on our lives. For example, if you feel overwhelmed, probably half of those problems you listed are actually inconsequential. Like, grouping your looming work deadline in with picking up the dry cleaning and making dinner. Those two things are not life or death situations, and really, neither is that deadline.

Next, think about the worst-case scenario for your failures to meet this deadline. What can you do to increase productivity? Make yourself a schedule? Enlist the help of other co-workers? Do you need to pick up the dry cleaning today, or is tomorrow better? How about just picking something up for dinner on the way home?

While this was a pretty straight forward example, other emotions are certainly more complicated to manoeuvre. However, if you use the same kind of framework to rationalise your emotions as above, the result can be the same. Also, don't forget to consider your body's physical reactions to certain situations. If you are not sure why your stomach is sick when you are in a particularly stressful situation, this is your body telling you that something is wrong, the physical manifestation of emotion. Don't ever ignore these signals. Your body and your inner self know you better than you do, so it is vitally important to consider these cues to navigate your life.

Don't expect to be able to rationalise your emotions within just a few minutes of meditation. Sometimes it takes a lifetime of self-awareness to make sense of something you are feeling. Don't let that be discouraging. There is plenty of time, and as long as you make an effort to understand your emotions, you are headed in the right direction.

With acute emotions, like getting angry about something in the moment, it takes a little bit more skill to manoeuvre. We have all been there. A car cuts us off in traffic, or someone says something that just cuts to the core. At the moment, you feel your face flush and anger boil up inside of you. It takes all of your willpower not to lash out at them.
In these moments, it is crucial to practice self-awareness and do a split-second analysis of your feelings. Start this process off by taking one big deep breath, in and out. With your exhale goes a bunch of pent up energy that is just waiting to burst. Next, think quickly about what has just occurred. Were you truly offended or have your feelings been blown out of proportion?

Next, think about how you will feel after you have given that car the finger or reamed out this person for what they have said. You may feel validated for a quick second, but the negativity of your bad reaction will linger with you much longer. This step allows you to curb your reaction to avoid personally feeling worse later on.

If you simply do not know what to do, do nothing. It is better to take some more time to react to a situation than it is to overreact at the moment. Yes, a witty comeback to a snarky comment may make you feel on top of things at the moment. But remember, taking some time to reflect on where this altercation had come from may make you realise that this person never meant to be rude, or if they did, that it is coming from a place of self-consciousness, anger, and insecurity. Perpetuating those feelings only bring negativity to life, and nothing good. Responding negatively only brings more problems your way.

You may have noticed in the past that your common reactions to stressful situations, like an argument, is to one-up people. That is, have the last word, and cut to the core just to feel like you have won. What has this gotten you?

Lastly, if you have chosen the high road, and did not choose to respond to this acute stressful situation, take sometime later to reflect on your true feelings. Were you really mad at that car for cutting you off, or did that just push you over the edge on top of being stressed about work? Would that person really have deserved a lashing via car window, or were they just trying to merge with traffic?

Putting some time between you and the situation gives the brain time to make sense of the emotions logically. Perhaps you made a rash decision in the heat of the moment and lashed out at your coworker who made a nasty comment. You may have responded with something just as rude, and you are now regretting it. Things may not have gone that well, but it can certainly be a learning moment. Explore the feelings you had before, during and after this altercation to learn a bit more about your emotional patterns.

For instance, if you recognise that you had been stressed about something else before this conversation began, you were already in a heightened state of agitation. Understand what it feels like for you to be stressed, so that when it happens again (and it certainly will), you will be able to sense it and take steps to calm yourself before continuing.

Think about the comment that was said. Was it truly nasty or was it meant to be a sort of constructive criticism from your co-worker? This really could go both ways, but if you had not been agitated, to begin with, do you think you would still have been offended? If you would have been, would making a nasty remark back really make you feel better? Resolve the situation, or just make things worse?

Reflecting on all of these things after the moment has passed trains your brain to think about things logically, instead of just stewing about the encounter afterwards. As your mind gets used to doing this constantly, it will be able to think this way very quickly at the moment with some practice. Rather than going over what you could have said in return to infinity in your mind, do something constructive and pick apart your feelings about the event instead.

Whether you are new to getting in touch with your feelings or if you are an old pro (nobody is) it helps to get an outside opinion. While you should learn to trust your gut feelings, it can help to consult with someone outside the situation, who can see above all of the feelings to see the logic. For example, imagine that you are in a new relationship and you are head over heels for your new partner and really want things to work out, everything seems perfect. Yet, you have a nagging feeling that something is not quite right.

While you may not be able to make a valid conclusion on your own, consulting with a friend who has your best interests in mind may be able to shed some light on some suspicious behaviour that has been bothering you. Instead of ignoring your suspicions for the sake of hoping the relationship works, your friend may be able to knock some sense into you if something is really off. Don't be afraid to consult with others if you cannot quite make sense of your feelings, and even if you cannot find a logical reason or cause for the emotion, don't just dismiss it. The emotion is not happening for nothing, you just may not be able to find that reason yet.

As you practice these techniques, you will become more emotionally confident, in that you will quickly be able to understand what you are feeling and react appropriately, as you are in touch with those feelings. This takes a great deal of regular practice, and new situations will always be emerging. Consciously take part in your emotional health every day, at any given moment. Squashing feelings to deal with later only brings on more trouble.

Being on top of your emotions constantly can be very draining and counter-productive. Bad feelings are meant to propel you to make changes, some of which you may not be ready for. It can be mentally exhausting to feel like you need to feel happy and content constantly, so give yourself a break. If work stresses you out, it is okay to live with that feeling for a little bit until you have the strength and wherewithal to handle making a change.

3 | MANAGE YOUR LIFE WITH EMOTIONAL INTELLIGENCE

As we learned in the second chapter, it is vitally important that we take time to pick apart and really comprehend what we are feeling. It is then, and only then, may we react in a way that is true to ourselves. With our example in the first chapter, we find that it is very easy to make quick, rash decisions when our emotions are high. Often, we regret our actions later on, as our minds logically process our thoughts and feelings after the fact.

Emotions can be very effective teaching and guidance tools if we use them properly. You may feel that in the past, your emotions bring you nothing but trouble. In reality, our bodies feel emotions to help lead us in the right direction. We feel fear or anxiety if we are in a situation that is dangerous or at least undesirable. We feel happy and content when we are safe and sound. Physiologically speaking, our emotions can keep us out of trouble by sounding the alarm when things are not quite right. Emotions can indicate when to turn and run from a bad situation, whether that be a relationship or job title. The reality of life requires us to think with our emotions and our minds in tandem to avoid completely derailing ourselves.

As our brains have something logical to say about our emotions, we often stay in bad circumstances or miss out on moments of happiness for the sake of moving along. In the grand scheme of things, it is important to be happy. We should follow the guidance of our inner selves to figure out what we want to do, where we want to be, and who we want to be with.

It is possible to manage what happens in our life by using our emotional intelligence. Let's say you have a job that you are not very thrilled with. The hours are long, your co-workers do not see eye to eye with you, but the money is good. This compels you to stay, as financial security is what your logical mind thinks. A job opportunity arises with a company that has more flexible hours, but less pay. Intrigued, you take an interview and find that you seem to mesh with the group.

What follows is a struggle between your brain's logic, and your emotional intelligence, which is only guided by your inner self, and it is the idea of happiness (a novel approach). While the decision may not always be so black and white, it seems obvious to go for a job that will give you more time to do things you love and to work in a more hospitable environment. Yet, what holds you back is the logic of financial unknown. Seeing this scenario from outside of it makes it easy to make a decision, but as you are engrossed in it, you may not have so much clarity. Allow your emotions to play a part in your decisions, but remember to use your logic as well.

We must become more open to our emotions to get what we truly want out of life. In the realm of self-help, the idea of our inner self, or spirit comes up quite a bit. If you subscribe to this theory, the idea is that each of us has an inner spirit that is guided by energy. The physical universe is also made of energy, and at its very core are the positive and negative charges that are responsible for all physical reactions and we are all part of this energy field. That part is pure physics.
With this, we are meant to take the path of least resistance (as physics proves) to interact with energy around us. This is much like lightning striking the tallest tower to reach the ground.

Many self-help gurus have taken this scientific idea and created a metaphor for life. In life, we will constantly be bombarded with decisions. If we make those choices by the guidance of our inner spirit, following emotional cues and gut feelings, our path will be met with less resistance. You have likely seen this before. Think about the ease in which you do something you like and are passionate about, versus doing things you don't like. The idea that time flies when you are having fun is a perfect example here.

However, our logic often goes against our emotions and pulls us further away. As we stray from the path, our inner selves try to lead us back in the right direction. By throwing negative emotions and obstacles in our way, our inner self, or gut feelings tries to deter us when we are making bad decisions, and lead us back to the path of least resistance.

By considering our logic, we can stay true to our beliefs and morals, something our emotions may easily forget. Think about the job decision again. The universal obstacles in the first job include the long hours, exhaustion, and difficult working conditions. Listening to your gut, and your inner self, you will see that the second, lower-paying job will get you closer to happiness, and had you simply squashed those emotions you would fail to experience how life would be with this job.

It is your choice whether you decide to take an opportunity or squander it. Perhaps you have been drawn to this job because of the convenience it will give you, or something else. Regardless, you can recognise an opportunity when you see one. But maybe you are too nervous about the money to trust your instincts and make a move. Now the moment has passed. You had a chance to become closer to happiness, and you may have made the wrong decision. Not to worry, there is always something to learn from a mistake, and this knowledge can be used to strike at opportunities in the future, that is if you choose to learn from it.

Using these emotional cues and learning from your wins and failures is a smart way to manage your life. The problem with mastering it is that everyone's emotions and experiences are different. No two people will learn the same way, or have the same opportunities. Our inner selves are all different, striving for different definitions of happiness.

Therefore, it is hard to tell you exactly how to follow your emotions. What can help are a few tangible activities to help you get in better touch with things. Journaling can be a powerful tool in helping you sort through and understand your emotions. Writing down what you are feeling, or even keeping a video or voice journal can help you.

Writing things down or saying them out loud puts a tangibility to your feelings. Rereading the entry after it is written is like reading a textbook guide to your feelings. You may only feel stressed or upset or happy in a fleeting moment, but if you can revisit the recount of the feelings, it can help you better understand. Getting the emotions down on paper can help remove them from you. Once you have some distance between you and a deep emotional response, it is easier to make a rational decision. Being very angry or anxious in a particular moment could lead us to make a rash decision, even if we feel highly compelled and confident in the moment. Again, be careful to distinguish between brain rational and spirit rational, as it is easy to get these confused.

As you recount your journal, you are looking to read between the lines and determine what it is that you are having trouble with. For example, if you were to write about the decision to take a new job, it might look something like this:

I have the opportunity to work for XYZ company, something I have been keeping my eye on. It seems really great to make my own hours, and the people there seem really easy to work with. If I take this job, it would mean I could take time in the morning to exercise and make breakfast for the kids before dropping them off to school. It would also make it a lot easier to cut out early if someone gets sick or there is an event I want to go to.

If I stay with ABC company, I will be able to save enough money to send the kids to college and take a great family vacation. But, I will still be stuck with the same long hours and stress. I dread going to work most days because I can't seem to fit in with my team.

What is the underlying theme of the entry? If you look closely, this decision really isn't about the job, as the actual work was not discussed at all. The priority here is family and quality of life. Now read the two paragraphs separately. Reading the first one, there is an air of lightness, hope, and promise. The second seems dark and dingy. How does reading each paragraph make you feel? How does the thought of working for ABC company affect your emotional well-being?

Using emotional intelligence, we can rationally sort through the emotions that underlie certain decisions. Of course, this day and age we need to consider the feelings of our spouses, children and anyone else that could be affected by the decision (see the next chapter), but beyond anything, our happiness should be the first priority. While that sounds a bit selfish, if you are happy, your relationships with others will be better and stronger, and everyone will benefit in the long run. In the next chapter, we will discuss a bit more about how to express these feelings to get others to understand, so they can be on board with your decision making.

4 | UNDERSTANDING EMOTIONS IN OTHERS

While it is vital to understand your own emotional status by practising self-awareness, our social and professional lives would be lacking if we did not completely understand the emotions of others. Everything is built around relationships with other people. You cannot carry out a romantic relationship with someone you do not get, or have a successful professional career unless you interact well with others. For many, being social is a regular part of the day. Little thought is required to make conversation or be in tune with the needs of others.

For the majority of us, however, these skills are highly lacking, and it can be a struggle just to have a basic conversation with another, let alone be aware of how they are feeling and reacting to you. We often get so bogged down in our own agenda and thinking of things to say that we are not paying attention to the subtle clues that people give to show how they are feeling.

Our brains are wired to figure these things out through the use of mirrored neurons in the brain. These act to see, hear and sense social cues so that we may better understand our friends and family. Without this, we would all be acting on our impulses, with little regard for the well-being of others. It is with knowing what makes people angry and sad that has driven the societal rules we currently have in place.

Your first clue of how a conversation is going is to monitor what it is your partner is saying, as well as how they are saying it. For example, if you are talking about the weather with a complete stranger in an elevator, you can determine a lot from such a short interaction. Is the person engaged in the conversation, or just responding simply to your remarks? If a person answers your questions with a simple yes or no, they are likely not interested in furthering the conversation. The interpretation of why is a layer deeper, which you may not have the opportunity to explore.

If an interaction with a close friend goes the same way, there is room to figure out how they are feeling. If this really is a good buddy, simply asking what's up is a great place to start. If they trust you, they might have already plan to tell you what is on their mind. Some friends can be a bit aloof, and a bit of guesswork is necessary.

If your counterpart is unwilling to actually tell you how they are feeling, rely on body language to help you figure it out. You can tell when most people are sad or upset, as they tend to slouch over, avoid eye contact and the like.

You may be thinking that it would just be easier to mind your own business and worry about yourself. While this may keep you out of some unnecessary drama, disconnecting yourself from close loved ones and friends will affect your life. Choosing to ignore emotions and not getting involved in those feelings will isolate you and affect your social life, as well as your work life.

Ironically, a good way to begin changing how you interpret someone else's emotions is by disconnecting from them a bit. For example, you may interpret a friend blowing you off as personally offensive, just as most people would. Instead of letting your feelings spiral into anger and questions about your self-worth, you need to disconnect and try and find a logical solution to the events that have arisen. Maybe this person is stuck in traffic, and their phone is dead. Maybe they had an emergency and could not contact you to reschedule your rendezvous.

Before you get defensive and leave them a nasty voicemail, consider these things. That message could go from nasty and friendship-ending to a nice one hoping they are okay, and to call back when they can. You never know what another person is going through, so it is best to treat them with kindness and respect until they give you a real reason to end the friendship.

Giving people the benefit of the doubt and assuming that they have the best intentions is good practice. Be positive and always try to consider both sides of a situation before reacting negatively. If someone cuts you off in traffic, think about how he or she might be late for work, and if they are late again, they might be fired. They need that spot in line more than you do. Most importantly, people make mistakes, and sometimes you just need to let it go.

Professionally, the hardest-hit people are those that work by word of mouth, like a doctor, therapist or dietitian. Their job is to talk to people, understand how they are feeling physically and emotionally, and make recommendations based on emotion. Outside of that, their business will be driven by word of mouth and making positive connections in the community. Sure, going to business chamber meetings will get you a few new clients, creating relationships by investing in the emotional well-being of another will drive your business to a level you had never imagined.

The only way to connect with someone on an emotional level is to have empathy for their situation. Examine how you would be feeling in a similar situation. For example, going back to the work situation, imagine if you were asked to work late on a whim, and you were upset about it. Maybe it is not that you are lazy and uncommitted, but that you are exhausted and need a break from the project. Being asked to cast aside other responsibilities to work late is annoying, and you already give enough of your time during the week.

Seeing things from this angle helps you be a better manager. If you can understand where someone is coming from, you can make better decisions, and even if your employees still absolutely need to work late, you can empathise and compensate them for their time and dedication.
Knowing how someone else is feeling is always a complicated matter. In essence, you can never really know how someone feels because his or her emotions are their own. You do not have the

same life knowledge that they do. Therefore, your perspective of any given situation will likely not be the same. Instead of insisting that you can see it from their angle, try creating an open dialogue in which they can express those feelings so that you may better comprehend them.

This does not mean having a deep-rooted therapy session every time a conflict arises, but simply asking for a person's thoughts before drawing your own conclusions is good practice. Start the conversation with verbiage like "How would you feel if…" or "Would it be too bold to ask…." This gives the person the opportunity to speak up for themselves, an opportunity that is simply demanding or stating a fact does not present.

5 | CHANGING EMOTIONS IN OTHERS

By recognising and comprehending emotions, it is possible to manage people. However, there is a very fine line between persuasion and manipulation, and trying to alter the emotions of another walks that line. The idea of mind control is a novel one. If only we could be so persuasive that people do what we wanted all the time! Sure that sounds great, but this is not ethical. Manipulating people into feeling guilty or sorry for you is not what this chapter intends. Instead, using emotional intelligence to help interact with people can improve the quality of your life and get you ahead professionally.

The fact that you can understand another person's emotions poises you for a better relationship with that person. Romantic or friendly relationships are a great example. If you can empathise with the wishes of a friend, it can make you a more attentive, meaningful friend in return.

For example, let's say your spouse has had a terrible day at work. You know this because they called you upset and ready to quit. Your remarkable ability to pick up on this anger (it is pretty obvious in this case) helps you decide how to act. You have one of two choices. You can either empathise with them, change your plans and try to make them feel better, or you could be selfish and go out with your friends, leaving your spouse at home to stew with their work problem alone.

Having a good emotional connection and being on the same plane as someone is the key to happy, healthy relationships. Understanding people on a more personal level builds trust and confidence, which shine through in good times and in bad.

Emotional intelligence can assist you in the climb to the top of the corporate ladder as well. Understanding how another person views things can help you persuade them. This is a valuable tool in just about any aspect of the business. For example, if your boss is due to promote someone in the office and you know what kind of work ethic and skills that he values, you can use this information to play up your strengths. If your boss personally believes that you hold the same values and emotions, a stronger bond can be formed, which could lead to your promotion.

In sales, emotions are constantly worked. Cars and other big-ticket items are no longer sold because they have x, y and z features. Now, commercials and sales pitches are geared toward the feeling a car can evoke. For a minivan, commercials aim to promote safety, security, and reliability, but not by saying the car is safe, secure and reliable, but through some backward subliminal advertising with a perfect, happy family driving the car safely to soccer practice. On the flip side, a convertible is sold with images of the open road, wind in your hair and the essence of freedom. Most businesses have learned to capitalise on the emotional strings of their consumers.

To truly persuade someone by playing on their emotions, you must be fully committed to their well-being. There are plenty of manipulative people out there who just want to sell their product or get something out of people, and that is not what this is about. Instead, we need to look at the ability to form a long-standing, healthy relationship with another person. You must be interested, engaged and willing to put in the work of trying to figure out their emotional cues. This comes with time, and much practice, just like working on your own thoughts.

Make your relationships off auto-pilot. Delve deeper into the shallow relationships that you have. Yes, you may bond over golf with a friend, as that is something that you have in common. While you are out on the course try engaging them in more personal conversation, instead of the usual play banter (just don't do this in their back swing). A great way to get someone to open up and share some feelings is to go first. Say something about how the trees on the course remind you of the old neighbourhood where you grew up, and how you and your siblings used to play in those trees. The conversation will fail if you try to go too deep, too soon, so just try a little bit at a time. A simple, reminiscent moment like this can lead to questions about where they grew up, what kinds of things they used to do, so on and so on.

This is not rocket science, it is just vigilance. Stop living out your relationships on the outskirts and really get to know somebody. Granted, this person may not be so emotionally intelligent themselves, but everyone has to start somewhere. At any given moment, you should be able to tap into the thoughts and feelings of yourself and another. All it takes is a little break from the rat race to consider feelings and act by good will.

CONCLUSION

Thank you for making it through to the end of Emotional Intelligence: Be Mindful. I hope it was informative and able to provide you with all of the tools you need to achieve your goals of enhancing your emotional connections.

The next step is to consciously make an effort to delve into your emotions, and to understand the feelings and thoughts of others better. Doing so will enhance all aspects of your life, and could bring about changes that will propel you into new adventures you never expected.

Do you think you can help me out?

If you found this book useful in any way, a review on Amazon is always appreciated, even if it's one line. Reviews really do help indie authors like me reach new readers.

Please head over to the following web link to post your quick short review www.rebrand.ly/review-ei

Thank you for your support.

OTHER BOOKS BY LEWIS

1) Anxiety Management: Reclaiming Your Life
2) Self Discipline: Develop Willpower & Become More Disciplined
3) Growth Mindset: The Door To Achieving More
4) Self-Esteem Improvement: Get Your Confidence Back
5) Weight Loss: Effective Weight Loss Ideas & Healthy Diet Recipes

Printed in Great Britain
by Amazon